ideals®
MOTHER'S DAY

More Than 50 Years of Celebrating Life's Most Treasured Moments

Vol. 53, No. 3

"The world has no such flower in any land, and no such pearl in any gulf or sea, as a babe on a mother's knee."

—Algernon Charles Swinburne

IDEALS—Vol. 53, No. 3 May MCMXCVI IDEALS (ISSN 0019-137X) is published eight times a year: February, March, May, June, August, September, November, December by IDEALS PUBLICATIONS INCORPORATED, 535 Metroplex Drive, Suite 250, Nashville, TN 37211. Second-class postage paid at Nashville, Tennessee, and additional mailing offices. Copyright © MCMXCVI by IDEALS PUBLICATIONS INCORPORATED. POSTMASTER: Send address changes to Ideals, PO Box 305300, Nashville, TN 37230. All rights reserved. Title IDEALS registered U.S. Patent Office.

SINGLE ISSUE—U.S. $5.95 USD; Higher in Canada
ONE-YEAR SUBSCRIPTION—8 issues—U.S. $19.95 USD; Canada $36.00 CDN (incl. GST and shipping); Foreign $25.95 USD
TWO-YEAR SUBSCRIPTION—16 issues—U.S. $35.95 USD; Canada $66.50 CDN (incl. GST and shipping); Foreign $47.95 USD

Printed and bound in USA. Printed on Weyerhaeuser Husky.

The paper used in this publication meets the minimum requirements of American National Standard for Information Sciences—Permanence of Paper for Printed Library Materials, ANSI Z39.48-1984.

Unsolicited manuscripts will not be returned without a self-addressed, stamped envelope.

ISBN 0-8249-1135-0   GST 131903775

Cover Photo: A SUNDAY RIDE. Al Riccio.

Inside Front Cover: IRIS GARDEN. David Schatz, artist. Courtesy of the artist and Wild Wings, Inc., Lake City, Minnesota.

Inside Back Cover: FEMME ET ENFANT AU JARDIN by Edouard Vuillard, 1868-1940. Superstock.

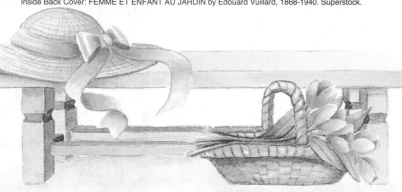

Song:
On May Morning

John Milton

Now the bright morning star, day's harbinger,
Comes dancing from the east and leads with her
The flowery May, who from her green lap throws
The yellow cowslip and the pale primrose.
Hail, bounteous May, that dost inspire
Mirth and youth and warm desire;
Woods and groves are of thy dressing,
Hill and dale doth boast thy blessing.
Thus we salute thee with our early song
And welcome thee and wish thee long.

AZALEAS AND DOGWOODS
Missouri Botanical Garden
Gay Bumgarner

Spring Celebration

George R. Kossik

When I see the golden glory
    As the sun begins to rise
And the splendor of the heavens
    In the far-off, eastern skies;

When I hear the songbirds singing
    As the night turns into day
With fresh dewdrops for their drinking
    From the blossoms when it's May;

When the breeze blows soft and gentle
    With the scent of sweet perfume
And the hummingbirds are busy,
    Feasting fast upon the bloom;

Then with songs and hymns and praises
    To creation's Lord and King,
I, with birds and blooms and breezes,
    Celebrate the lovely spring.

ROSE TRELLIS—HUMMINGBIRDS
Susan Bourdet, artist
Courtesy of the artist and Wild Wings, Inc.
Lake City, Minnesota

Overleaf Photograph
SPRING GARDEN
Southeastern Pennsylvania
G. Hampfler/H. Armstrong Roberts

"I was always a lover
of soft-winged things."

—Victor Hugo

The Robin's Song

Kay Hoffman

I heard him sing at early dawn
His happy, lilting, wake-up song.
How can he sing, I pondered, when
The sky is dark, the day yet dim?

And then I thought a bird so small
Is wiser than we humans all
To put all trust in God's great care;
It matters not skies dark or fair.

I humbly bowed my head to pray,
"God, keep me in your care today."
His presence seemed so very near;
I sensed the robin's source of cheer.

When skies are dark or when they're fair,
I've come to trust His loving care.
In soft, gray mist of early dawn,
God touched me with the robin's song.

O Child

C. Haney

O child who waits by yesterday's gate,
I see you touch the blossom on the vine
That twines about the aged wood;
I see your small nose plunge gently into
Its scented depth. I see you laughing,
Gleeful as you catch the colorful confetti
Of petals that rains gently down upon you
From blossom-laden branches above.

And like nature, you cannot be caught
Standing still. I see you bending, scooping,
Chasing butterflies and birds; I see you
Running, jumping, and reaching for the sky,
The clouds, the tops of trees and, at last,
Choosing forget-me-nots for your precious bouquet.

O child, as you turn to greet me, you
Lead me, show me, coax me to see
My garden once again through your eyes;
To see each day a garden is a newly
Discovered haven. A garden is ever growing,
Ever changing, ever new;
And forever, a garden is a gift of love to be shared.

IN THE GARDEN
Barbara Peacock
FPG International

BITS & PIECES

Sometimes the strength of motherhood is greater than natural laws.

—*Barbara Kingsolver*

My mother is a poem I'll never be able to write, though everything I write is a poem to my mother.

—*Sharon Doubiago*

When Mama smiled, beautiful as her face was,
it grew incomparably more lovely, and everything around seemed brighter.

—*Leo Tolstoy*

Mama! Dearest Mama!
I know you are my one
true friend.

—*Nikolai Gogol*

A mother is . . . different from anything else
that God ever thought of. . . . She is a distinct
and individual creation.

—*Henry Ward Beecher*

The sweetest sounds to mortals given are heard in
mother, home, and heaven.

—*W. G. Brown*

Such a beautiful word in the language we know,
Which in memory exceeds any other,
Is the word that brings joy to the eyes of us all;
It's the word of the universe—mother.

—*Harriet Elmblad*

Morning Gold

Elva McAllaster

Floral beauty
on my breakfast table
blesses
this early spring day.

Not, this time,
a potted cyclamen or freesia;
not, this time,
a rose or a carnation
from the florist shelves.

Here crisp green spears
of dandelion leaves
(transplanted, for now, into kitchen ceramic)
and small gold dandelion suns
that gleam and glow—

Suns lighting up
a cloud-dark sky, horizon wide;
suns lighting up
one gladdened heart.

HANDMADE HEIRLOOM

❖ ❖ ❖

KNITTED DEDICATION BLANKET. Knitted by Mary Skarmeas. Jerry Koser Photography.

KNITTED DEDICATION BLANKET

Mary Skarmeas

Knitting has always been my favorite craft. It is both practical and endlessly varied. I can try new patterns, new yarns, new stitches, new textures; and the result is always something that has a ready-made place in my own life or, more often than not, in the life of the special someone who is the object of my needles' work.

The most intense incentive to knit something beautiful comes, for me, when a new baby is on the way. I love to knit baby things. They are so small and dainty and soft, and they progress quickly. Knitting for a new grandchild is all the more compelling—a true labor of love. Since I learned that a second grandchild will soon be filling my life with joy, my needles have not just been clicking, they have been flying.

Knitting is one of the oldest crafts known to civilization. It dates back thousands of years and is believed to have begun in Egypt. Over time, the craft made its way to Europe and the British Isles where, during the Middle Ages, knitting was considered the sole domain of men—a woman's job was to spin the wool into yarn. Accomplished knitters joined together in knitters' guilds, and young men wishing to become knitters served apprenticeships to learn techniques and patterns. Only after completing such training and demonstrating a high level of skill and creativity were apprentice knitters considered for guild membership. The master knitters of the guilds created their own patterns and distinctive garments and were commissioned by nobility and royalty, just as were the finest tailors and dressmakers. The sailors and fishermen of the British Isles, using skills needed for tying intricate rope knots and making and repairing nets, became particularly adept at knitting the warm, woolen sweaters ideal for their days at sea. These fisherman-knit sweaters are still popular across the world.

Of course, times changed; and women eventually took over the bulk of the world's hand-knitting. Knitting gave mothers the ability to make warm, woolen garments for their families; in cold climates it was an essential skill for every homemaker. The mere necessity of the items that knitters produced guaranteed that the craft would never go out of style. Even when new fabrics and machines made hand-knitting less a necessity and more of a leisure-time art, knitting never lost its practical appeal. Today, while one can certainly purchase machine-knit woolen items of every shape, size, and color, there remains something truly special about a quality hand-knit; it is this truth that keeps so many knitters devoted to their beloved craft.

Knitting is, at its heart, a simple craft. There are only a handful of basic stitches and techniques to learn—the challenge and the variety come in the endless number of stitch combinations, the ever-changing selection of yarn colors, types, and textures, and the increasing dexterity that comes with practice. As an accomplished knitter, I know that even the patterns that bring exclamations of disbelief from nonknitting admirers are truly very simple. It is all a matter of mastering a few basic stitches and following directions. It is also a matter of comfort. Like any new skill, knitting feels awkward to hands unused to holding and moving the needles, but perseverance will make those needles feel like extensions of your own hands.

The best way to start knitting is to find someone who knits and ask for help. Learning needle position and stitches from the pictures in a book is hard; it is far better to have someone demonstrate with their own work and offer advice and encouragement along the way. Once you have been guided through your first project by an experienced knitter, you will be ready to move ahead and learn and experiment on your own. If you don't have a friend or family member who knits, just walk into a local yarn store; more often than not there is someone there very willing to get a new knitter started.

Knitting lends itself well to producing heirlooms. These heirlooms are of a different type, of course, than a china cup or a porcelain doll. A hand-knit sweater, no matter how lovingly cared for, will not last forever, but neither will it sit on a shelf collecting dust. The cherished, handmade sweater or afghan is a living, breathing heirloom, one that will become a part of daily life, ritual, and tradition. With today's wonderful, durable selection of yarns—from the traditional wools to washable wools, cottons, blends, and even synthetics—hand-knits that are cared for properly can last several lifetimes. When at last they have seen their final days, they will bid farewell to a full and involved life.

My current project is a dedication blanket for our new grandchild. This afghan is knit in sparkling white to cuddle the child in a grandmother's warm love on a special day. Working on this afghan has reminded me of one of the great joys of knitting. Knitting is a quiet, calming craft, one that leads to daydreaming and planning for the future. Each stitch brings thoughts of the gift's recipient—in this case a baby without a face or a name, but one who has already won my heart.

I intend to embroider the afghan with the baby's name and date of birth. Our new little one will not remember his or her dedication day, but my hope is that someday my grandson or granddaughter will pick up this lovely white afghan, read the embroidered name, and remember the warmth of a grandmother's unconditional love. In the grandest sense, knitting this afghan gives me a measure of immortality. Perhaps some day it will wrap my great-grandchild on another dedication day; if it does, I will be there.

Mary Skarmeas lives in Danvers, Massachusetts, and has recently earned her bachelor's degree in English at Suffolk University. Mother of four and grandmother of two, Mary loves all crafts, especially knitting.

The Mother-to-be

Lolita Pinney

She walks in a glory delightful to see,
Most blessed of women—the mother-to-be.
Her days are enchanted, caught up in a spell.
She's kin to an angel; with her, smiles dwell.
Her arms have a look while folded at rest
As though they await a small, welcome guest.

Her body is growing (a girl or a boy?)
As tangible proof of her heart's greatest joy:
A baby to cuddle, caress, and to teach.
A lifetime of longing is just within reach—
A twenty-year task, a great labor of love,
A bonus of blessing sent down from above.

Her eyes shine with dream dust no mortal has seen;
An invisible halo she wears like a queen.
A mission of motherhood God's grace has willed;
Now waiting and confident, she is fulfilled.
His radiant promise, in her, one can see,
Most blessed of women—the mother-to-be.

WAITING FOR SISTER
Superstock

THROUGH MY WINDOW

Pamela Kennedy

Art by Russ Flint

MOTHERS-IN-WAITING

I think it is very appropriate that mothers spend nine months waiting for the birth of a child. It is this period of time that serves to prepare a mother for what she will be doing for much of the rest of her children's lives—waiting.

No one ever explained this fact to me before I had children. I read books about feeding and disciplining, about first aid and toilet training, but none of them contained even a chapter about waiting. This meant I had to blaze my own trail through the waiting rooms of motherhood—a particularly inefficient way of doing business. For this reason, I think at least a rudimentary guide to waiting is long overdue for expectant mothers.

The underlying truth women need to understand before they ever embark on the adventure of motherhood is this: waiting is an aspect of parenting that not only seems endless, it actually is endless. Although waiting begins before birth, it doesn't end with the arrival of your little one. No, it just moves on down the track to the next station.

Once you've made it through labor and delivery, another kind of waiting begins. It is what I like to call "developmental waiting." The new mother hovers around her little offspring while eagerly anticipating any indications that she has produced another Einstein or the next Mozart. The first smile, the first tooth, the first focused stare are all interpreted as signs of early or, horrors, late development. Mothers in shopping malls engage in carefully orchestrated conversations aimed at determining how advanced their little one is compared to his or her peers.

"I see your baby is very alert! How old is she?" one asks coyly. "Three months? How darling. My little Alfred here held his head up the day after he was born and could focus on his fingers at one week!" she preens, convinced Alfred has surpassed all other babies in brilliance. The other mother takes her baby home and anxiously watches for some sign that her child too is advanced. This is particularly unproductive waiting since most babies are programmed to do this stuff on some mysterious schedule known only to them and God. Certain overachieving mothers seem determined to beat this schedule, however, and try all sorts of things to hurry it along. I must admit to guilt in this department as I recall ordering a kit of materials aimed at teaching my two-year-old to read. I spent hours convincing him to *study* the flashcards, not eat them! In the end, he learned to act interested when I brought out the cards—a feat I considered almost as wonderful as reading.

Fortunately, this kind of waiting is limited primarily to first children. By the time you have a second, you don't have time to wait around for every little thing: "Oh, Honey, the baby just bit me. When did he get those teeth?"

First words and steps and so forth are cute and kind of fun to wait for, but the waiting that mothers both detest and excel in comes later. It's the kind of waiting you do during soccer practice and ballet lessons and in the offices of dentists and doctors and principals. If you are a mother who is gifted with organization, you are never without "waiting things." That is, you always have a project you can work on while you wait. I know one mother who crocheted an entire king-size bed coverlet during little league season. Of course she had three boys, and they all ended up in the championships; so she probably could have done pillow shams too if she had really tried! Some of us are less creative and end up reading loads of romance novels each year while we're sitting in the bleachers or the waiting room. Still others have the enterprising know-how to turn waiting into a profit-making venture. A friend of mine folded, stuffed, and addressed millions of flyers while periodically smiling and nodding at her peewee football star who never guessed his mom couldn't tell a forward pass from a drop kick.

As boring and mind-numbing as waiting for young children can be, it seems a breeze when compared with the waiting that mothers do when their teens head out on their own. It's accompanied by vivid flashes of imagination—blazing car crashes, screeching ambulances, endless white hospital corridors filled with whispered conversations. It intensifies all the senses so that mothers can hear a car door slam halfway down the block and see the lights of an approaching vehicle before it even rounds the corner. It is also the kind of waiting most often denied by mothers: "Oh, hello, Honey. Is it midnight already? I was just waxing the floor. Did you have a nice evening?"

Waiting is one of the things mothers do whether they want to or not. There is no escaping it. And don't count on ever getting past the waiting room as a mother. I have an entire set of quilted Christmas ornaments my mother made while she was waiting for me to give birth to our second son. Just the other day I received a letter from her. She wondered when we might consider retiring from the military and moving some place closer to home. After consulting with my husband, I wrote back the only answer I could: "Well, Mom, I guess we'll just have to wait and see!"

Pamela Kennedy is a freelance writer of short stories, articles, essays, and children's books. Wife of a naval officer and mother of three children, she has made her home on both United States coasts and currently resides in Honolulu, Hawaii. She draws her material from her own experiences and memories, adding highlights from her imagination to enhance the story.

"A sweet new blossom of humanity, freshly fallen from God's own home to flower on earth."

—Gerald Massey

Birth

Annie R. Stillman

Just when each bud was big with bloom
And as prophetic of perfume;
When spring with her bright horoscope
Was sweet as an unuttered hope—

Just when the last star flickered out
And twilight, like a soul in doubt,
Hovered between the dark and dawn,
And day lay waiting to be born—

Just when the gray and dewy air
Grew sacred as an unvoiced prayer
And somewhere through the dusk she heard
The stirring of a nested bird—

Four angels glorified the place:
Wan Pain unveiled her awful face;
Joy, soaring, sang; Love, brooding, smiled;
Peace laid upon her breast a child.

LE BERCEAU
Berthe Morisot, 1841-1895
Superstock

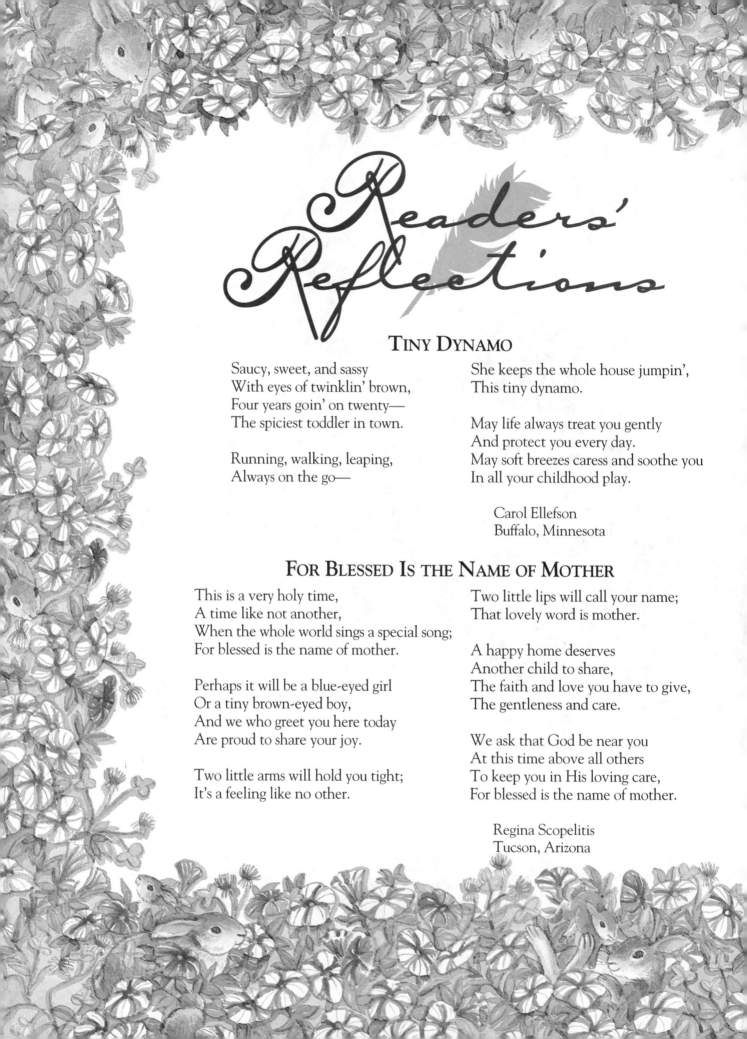

Readers' Reflections

TINY DYNAMO

Saucy, sweet, and sassy
With eyes of twinklin' brown,
Four years goin' on twenty—
The spiciest toddler in town.

Running, walking, leaping,
Always on the go—

She keeps the whole house jumpin',
This tiny dynamo.

May life always treat you gently
And protect you every day.
May soft breezes caress and soothe you
In all your childhood play.

Carol Ellefson
Buffalo, Minnesota

FOR BLESSED IS THE NAME OF MOTHER

This is a very holy time,
A time like not another,
When the whole world sings a special song;
For blessed is the name of mother.

Perhaps it will be a blue-eyed girl
Or a tiny brown-eyed boy,
And we who greet you here today
Are proud to share your joy.

Two little arms will hold you tight;
It's a feeling like no other.

Two little lips will call your name;
That lovely word is mother.

A happy home deserves
Another child to share,
The faith and love you have to give,
The gentleness and care.

We ask that God be near you
At this time above all others
To keep you in His loving care,
For blessed is the name of mother.

Regina Scopelitis
Tucson, Arizona

SUCCESSFUL

There are certain dreams I cherish
In the channels of my heart
That somehow seem more important
Every time a new day starts.
It's a feeling that comes to me
And can always top all others—
How to make myself successful
As a good, outstanding mother.

I may climb life's highest mountains,
I may gather wealth and fame,
They may list me with the greatest
Of the well-known, highbrow names.
But it all would have no meaning
If the test I didn't pass
And I failed to be successful
With my little lad and lass.

They are precious gifts God gave me
Just to make my life more bright,
And 'twill be my best ambition
That I set their footsteps right.
It's the one job that I dream of
And the biggest of all others
That I've got to be successful
As a good, outstanding mother.

Ruth J. Baker
Alliance, Ohio

A MOTHER'S BLESSING

When I was just little and had no cares,
I knew that my mother would always be there

With a touch warm and gentle,
A voice so serene,
And gentle persuasions like a guardian unseen.

And as I grew older,
She still was my strength,
Someone to confide in and talk to at length.

At her bedside I'd sit;
And the memories are sweet
As we talked away hours,
Our feelings complete.

What comfort! Those talks,
The quiet and peace,
Understanding to gain and confusion release.

And now I'm a mother,
But ever the more
Her words and her counsel help peace to restore.

Forever a mother, a sister, a friend—
To give daily sustenance till eternity's end.

Sandra Oliver Ferraro
Kaysville, Utah

A BABY

A baby is a precious gift
Sent from God above,
A complete and rich fulfillment
Of a man and woman's love.

A tiny little being
To cherish, love, and share

With husband, wife, and family
And all the friends who care.

A baby brings new life and hope
And hours of fun and laughter,
A new beginning, a fresh new start
For all our days hereafter.

Regina Racke
Pittsburgh, Pennsylvania

Riches

Elsie Pearson

If ever carelessly I've frowned
Upon this home of mine,
Forgetting all the lovesome things
A mother might enshrine

Within her heart; if I have sighed
For carpets wall-to-wall,
A dozen rooms, a spacious lounge,
A more imposing hall;

If I have sighed for silken gowns
And precious gems to wear
And phials of the rarest scents
And blossoms for my hair;

If I have hated for a while
The little, homely scenes,
The "making do" and "patching up"
That being mother means;

Forgive me, Lord, for in my heart
I know the things worthwhile.

Not all the precious gems on earth
Could buy my baby's smile.

Not all the gold could buy a curl,
Nor sapphire eyes of blue;
No pearls could buy one glistening tear
With laughter peeping through.

The texture of the richest silks,
Those silks for which I pine,
Could rival not a baby's skin,
So petal-soft and fine.

See here a precious treasure chest
I have not far to seek—
A fluffy dog is cuddled close
Against a rosy cheek,

In small, blue cot such wondrous wealth.
Come close and take a peep
And see the brightest gem I know—
My baby, fast asleep.

"A babe in a house is a wellspring of pleasure."

—Martin Farquhar Tupper

MOTHER AND SON
Edmund Blair Leighton
Superstock

MAY

Frank Dempster Sherman

May shall make the world anew;
 Golden sun and silver dew,
Money minted in the sky
 Shall the earth's new garments buy.

May shall make the orchards bloom;
 And the blossoms' fine perfume
Shall set all the honeybees
 Murmuring among the trees.

May shall make the bud appear
 Like a jewel, crystal clear,
Mid the leaves upon the limb
 Where the robin lilts his hymn.

May shall make the wildflowers tell
 Where the shining snowflakes fell;
Just as though each snowflake's heart,
 By some secret, magic art,

Were transmuted to a flower
 In the sunlight and the shower.
Is there such another, pray,
 Wonder-making month as May?

The unique perspective of Russ Flint's artistic style has made him a favorite of Ideals *readers for many years. A resident of California and father of four, Russ Flint has illustrated a children's Bible and many other books.*

MOM'S COOKIE JAR

Vivian Marie Chatman

The jar now stands upon my shelf
  In fondest memory
Of every cookie Mother baked
  Especially for me.
Her sugar cakes with cinnamon,
  With raisins, and with dates
Were sweets I munched on daily
  With the help of eager mates.

And when my world was troubled so,
  My face was washed with tears,
Mother gave me gingersnaps
  Then soothed away my fears.
And never was a single time
  When I was in her way,
When she wouldn't leave her kitchen,
  Shed her apron, come and play.

So finally her cookie jar
  Was given in my care,
A reminder from her always
  That in life we have to share
Our love, our time, our sweetest things
  With people passing through;
For joys you give to others
  Are the gifts life gives to you.

APRON STRINGS

Helen Welshimer

Two gingham strings to an apron,
　　But miniature cookies and pies
And scattered blocks and story hours
　　Were bound to the worn gingham ties.

A mother who put on an apron
　　Oft took time for you it seems
To sing of ports off eastern shores
　　And furnish the stories for dreams.

Two gingham strings to an apron,
　　But laughter and smiles and prayers
Were found in the gingham pockets,
　　Wrapped up with your childhood cares.

Two gingham strings to an apron,
　　But nobody ever knew
If she longed sometimes for a silken gown
　　When she put on an apron for you.

'Twas only a gingham apron,
　　But it pulls you wherever you roam;
For those apron strings were always worn
　　By a mother whose love warmed a home.

CORNER

COOKIE JARS

by Laura K. Griffis

Some of my most cherished childhood memories are of my grandmother always placing a delicious batch of homemade chocolate-chip cookies into her favorite cookie jar just before family gatherings. In the form of a grinning, green frog, this jar earned the nickname of "Croakie" from one of the grandchildren. According to a beloved family tradition, any grandchild who wanted a cookie had to approach the frog and say, "Croakie, Croakie, can I have a cookie?" With a wink and a smile, my grandmother would lean over and listen to Croakie's response. Croakie always said yes.

Cookie jars warm anyone's kitchen; perhaps because so many of us attach happy childhood memories to them. For those who collect cookie jars, the array of shapes and sizes provides a source of pleasure and nostalgia. For decades, pottery manufacturers have produced cookie jars for many purposes, from decorating a kitchen counter to commemorating an era in American history. The variety of cookie jars available to collectors reflects the diverse trends and familiar images of our culture.

Cookie jars are most likely distant cousins of the biscuit canisters popular in England during the nineteenth century. At teatime, an English hostess often served sweet tea biscuits, or cookies, in a decorative container. The trend soon found its way to America. During the 1930s, potteries in the Midwest began making jars of glass, ceramic, and tin in which cookies could be stored. As the years passed, cookie jars gained popularity and became available in a variety of creative styles.

The majority of sought-after cookie jars were produced during the 1950s or earlier. These jars exhibit a wide array of themes, including everything from storybook characters to grinning animals to commercial advertisements. When many American potteries closed their doors during the 1960s and 1970s, American cookie jars became instant collectibles. Today, they remain in high demand among cookie-jar enthusiasts.

The most valuable cookie jars were made by well-known potteries such as McCoy, American Bisque, and Brush Pottery. Often displaying distinguishing markings or colors, a common jar by one of these makers can often be worth up to one hundred dollars, although collectors are willing to pay prices into the thousands for the rarest jars.

Whereas a diligent collector can find jars of almost any theme, one of the most common motifs is popular

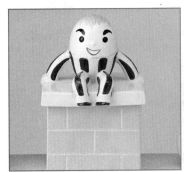

32

COLLECTIBLE COOKIE JARS. All images courtesy *Collector's Encyclopedia of Cookie Jars Book II*, by Fred and Joyce Roerig, Collector Books.

fictional characters. The jars that sport the nostalgic visages of Howdy Doody, Popeye, and Mickey Mouse are extremely collectible. However, more modern character jars, including those shaped as Winnie-the-Pooh and the Flintstones, were often produced in limited quantities and continue to grow in value. Appropriately enough, the furry blue form of Cookie Monster from "Sesame Street" also joined the cookie-jar menagerie. What child, or collector, could resist the lure of such lovable personalities?

If your interests lie in antique cookie jars, flea markets and garage sales often provide delectable finds. Check to see if the jar has undergone any repainting or repair, which can damage the original jar and its value. You can always keep an eye out for the marks of American potteries and mold numbers; yet expert collectors warn novices to be wary of spurious reproductions.

Some collectors choose to focus on new cookie jars and adhere to the adage that what is produced today is likely to become a collectible in the future. Department stores carry stylish selections from many of the well-known ceramics manufacturers, and beloved fictional characters continue to be popular choices. Years from now, perhaps the cookie jar you buy today will become as collectible as the rare Howdy Doody jar from decades ago.

Whether old or new, cookie jars are sure to brighten up your counter or add whimsy to your entire kitchen. Perhaps most of all, any jar you choose is certain to stir up fond memories of after-school snacks shared with Mom. As for me, I remain partial to my grandmother's "Croakie" jar and the batch of homemade chocolate-chip cookies nestling inside his belly!

A native of Texas, Laura K. Griffis is finishing her senior year at Vanderbilt University while working as an Ideals editorial intern. Laura collects postcards from her travels to museums around the world as a part of her ongoing study of international cultures.

My Place in Childhood

S. Lover

There was a place in childhood that I remember well,
And there a voice of sweetest tone bright fairy tales did tell;
And gentle words and fond embrace were given with joy to me
When I was in that happy place upon my mother's knee.

When fairy tales were ended, "good night," she softly said
And kissed and laid me down to sleep upon my tiny bed.
And holy words she taught me there; methinks I yet can see
Her angel eyes as close I knelt beside my mother's knee.

In the sickness of my childhood, the perils of my prime,
The sorrows of my riper years, the cares of every time,
When doubt and danger weighed me down, then pleading all for me,
It was a fervent prayer to heaven that bent my mother's knee.

Bedtime Blessing

James Neill Northe

May tree and plant
  and shrub
Be soundless
  through the night
And stars and moon
  be dimmed
To shut out
  all the light.

So when you sleep
  in peace,
No bird will move
  in flight,
And angels guard
  your sleep.
Good night, my love,
  good night.

A SLICE OF LIFE

Edgar A. Guest

WHEN MOTHER MADE AN ANGEL CAKE

When mother baked an angel cake,
　We kids would gather round
An' watch her gentle hands at work,
　An' never make a sound;
We'd watch her stir the eggs an' flour
　An' powdered sugar too
An' pour it in the crinkled tin,
　An' then when it was through,
She'd spread the icing over it,
　An' we knew very soon
That one would get the plate to lick
　An' one would get the spoon.

It seemed no matter where we were
　Those mornings at our play,
Upstairs or out of doors somewhere,
　We all knew right away

When Ma was in the kitchen
　An' was gettin' out the tin
An' things to make an angel cake,
　An' so we scampered in.
An' Ma would smile at us an' say:
　"Now you keep still an' wait
An' when I'm through I'll let you lick
　The spoon an' icing plate."

We watched her kneel beside the stove,
　An' put her arm so white
Inside the oven just to find
　If it was heatin' right.
An' mouths an' eyes were open then
　Because we always knew
The time for us to get our taste
　Was quickly comin' due.

Then while she mixed the icing up,
    She'd hum a simple tune,
An' one of us would bar the plate,
    An' one would bar the spoon.
Could we catch a glimpse of Heaven
    And some snow-white kitchen there,
I'm sure that we'd see Mother,
    Smiling now, and still as fair;

And I know that gathered round her
    We should see an angel brood
That is watching every movement
    As she makes an angel food;
For I know that little angels,
    As we used to do, await
The moment when she lets them lick
    The icing spoon and plate.

Edgar A. Guest began his illustrious career in 1895 at the age of fourteen when his work first appeared in the Detroit Free Press. *His column was syndicated in more than three hundred newspapers, and he became known as "The Poet of the People."*

Ideals' Family Recipes

Favorite Recipes from the Ideals Family of Readers

ALMOND PEACH MUFFINS

Preheat oven to 375° F. In a large bowl, sift together 1½ cups all-purpose flour, 1 cup granulated sugar, ¾ teaspoon salt, and ½ teaspoon baking soda; set aside. In a large bowl, combine 2 beaten eggs, ½ cup vegetable oil, ½ teaspoon vanilla extract, and ⅛ teaspoon almond extract. Add dry ingredients and stir just until moistened. Fold in ½ cup chopped almonds and 1¼ cups peeled, chopped peaches (or one 16-ounce can peaches, drained and chopped). Spoon batter into greased or paper-lined muffin cups until cups are three-fourths full. Bake 20 to 25 minutes. Cool in pan 10 minutes; remove to a wire rack. Makes 12 muffins.

Mrs. Sophia Boyer
York, Pennsylvania

NANNY'S CRANBERRY BREAD

Preheat oven to 350° F. In a large bowl, sift together 2 cups all-purpose flour, ¾ cup granulated sugar, 1 teaspoon baking soda, and 1 teaspoon salt. Set aside. In a large bowl, combine 1 egg, ⅔ cup milk, ½ cup chopped pecans or walnuts, and one 16-ounce can whole-berry cranberry sauce; mix well. Slowly add dry ingredients. Add ¼ cup melted butter; stir well. Spoon batter into a greased loaf pan. Bake 1 hour. Cool in pan. Makes 1 loaf.

Kathleen Roberts
St. Augustine, Florida

CUCUMBER SANDWICHES

Run the tines of a fork lengthwise down a large cucumber; slice and set aside to drain. Cut small rounds of rye or pumpernickel bread and spread with cream cheese. Place a cucumber slice on each round. Top with pimiento slices or sprigs of fresh dill. Makes approximately 2 dozen servings.

Sheri Dallas
Indianapolis, Indiana

RASPBERRIES AND CREAM

Preheat oven to 400° F. Place the shells from one 10-ounce package frozen puff pastry shells on an ungreased cookie sheet. Bake 20 to 25 minutes or until shells are golden brown and puffed. Place on wire rack to cool.

Wash and drain 2 cups fresh raspberries (or frozen berries may be used). Remove tops of shells and place 2 tablespoons of raspberries in each shell; reserve some berries for decoration. Mound each shell with non-dairy whipped topping. Garnish with remaining berries and arrange shell tops on serving dish. Makes 6 servings.

Kelly Hammond
Paris, Illinois

SPICED TEA

In a large saucepan, bring to a boil ½ cup water and ¾ cup granulated sugar. Remove from heat and add ¼ cup strained orange juice, ½ cup strained lemon juice, 6 whole cloves, and 1 cinnamon stick.

In a large, heated teapot, place 10 teaspoons orange pekoe tea leaves, either loose or in a tea ball. Add 5 cups boiling water. Cover, and permit tea to steep 3 to 5 minutes. Strain, or remove tea ball. Add cinnamon mixture. Serve at once. Makes eight 5-ounce servings.

Amy Jo Marks
Los Angeles, California

Editor's Note: Please send us your best-loved recipes! Mail a typed copy of the recipe along with your name, address, and telephone number to Ideals *magazine, ATTN: Recipes, P.O. Box 305300, Nashville, Tennessee 37230. We will pay $10 for each recipe used. Recipes cannot be returned.*

LEGENDARY AMERICANS

NANCY SKARMEAS

McRae

MARGARET RUDKIN

One popular story describes how Margaret Rudkin, the woman behind Pepperidge Farm bakeries, began her career as a means of helping her youngest son, Mark, who suffered from asthma. After the doctor suggested a chemical-free diet for young Mark, Rudkin was determined to make life better for her son and immediately went home to her kitchen to begin experimenting. The result was a loaf of whole-wheat bread so delicious and wholesome that, before long, Mrs. Rudkin had a growing business on her hands. Another version of the story describes how Rudkin, searching for ways to raise extra money after a serious accident temporarily disabled her husband, began baking bread and selling it to a local grocer. Rudkin herself offered little clarification. She once said that she began baking bread out of an "interest in proper food for children." Regardless of how she got her start, however, what cannot be denied is that within a few months of baking and selling her first loaf of bread, Margaret Rudkin was on her way to becoming one of the most successful businesswomen of her day.

Margaret Fogarty Rudkin was born in New York City in September of 1897. The eldest of five children, she spent her early childhood in Manhattan's Tudor City section, where she and her family shared a four-story brownstone with her Irish-born grandmother. When Margaret was twelve years old, the Fogartys moved to Flushing, on New York's Long Island, where Margaret eventually graduated as valedictorian of her high-school class and secured a job as a bookkeeper at a local bank.

The first woman hired by the bank, Margaret was committed to building a career for herself in the business world. She eventually left the bank for a better position at McClure, Jones and Company, a member of the New York Stock Exchange. Four years later, however, Margaret's plans changed when she met and married Henry Rudkin, a partner at McClure, Jones. After their marriage in 1923, Margaret left her job to devote her time to her new family. Over the next six years, the Rudkins added three sons to their family and moved out of Manhattan to a 125-acre estate in Fairfield, Connecticut, which they named Pepperidge Farm.

Like most women of her era who had the opportunity to enter the business world, Margaret Rudkin left behind her job to raise her family. Yet she did not leave behind her ambition, her intelligence, or her business sense. The Rudkins were a prosperous family. Their Pepperidge Farm estate included extensive stables, a collection of automobiles, and a cadre of household servants. When Henry Rudkin found himself temporarily out of work after the accident, the Rudkins were forced to give up many of their luxuries; but the family was by no means suffering financially, despite the depressed economy. Still, Margaret Rudkin, with her three boys of school age and time on her hands, began to think about ways of raising additional income for her family. She experimented with growing apples, then raising turkeys, and, in 1937, with baking bread.

Pepperidge Farm, Inc., began with a few loaves of whole-wheat bread sold to a local grocer in Fairfield. The recipe, quite likely developed with young Mark Rudkin's asthma in mind, was based on those recalled from Rudkin's early childhood and time spent in the kitchen with her Irish grandmother. What made Rudkin's bread special was that at a time when mass-produced, additive-laden baked goods were the norm, she used only fresh and wholesome ingredients—unbleached flour, fresh butter and eggs, and no chemical additives—and each loaf was kneaded by hand.

Within a few months, word of Rudkin's bread had spread through the area. The increased demand required that she move her baking operations from the kitchen to a renovated garage and bring in hired workers. White bread was soon added to the Pepperidge Farm product list; and Henry Rudkin, back at work in New York City, began delivering fresh loaves to Manhattan grocers who met him at Grand Central Station each morning.

Pepperidge Farm breads became the talk of the grocery world; and with the help of articles in newspapers and magazines, including one in *Reader's Digest* that produced orders for bread from throughout the United States and Canada, Margaret Rudkin's home bakery was soon a thriving, growing business. By 1940, only three years after selling her first loaf of bread, Margaret Rudkin was sending out fifty thousand loaves of bread each week from a new bakery in Norwalk, Connecticut. Eventually Henry Rudkin left his job on the Stock Exchange to help out with his wife's business; but Margaret remained the president of Pepperidge Farm, even after the company was sold in 1960.

Margaret Rudkin was a unique and inspirational figure, a devoted wife and mother, and also a skilled and ethical businesswoman. Perhaps the legend is true; perhaps she baked her first loaf of whole-wheat bread as a pure and selfless act of motherly devotion. It was this dedication along with her keen business savvy that led Rudkin to turn that first loaf into a thriving business. Based on a commitment to producing a good and wholesome product, Pepperidge Farm provided her family a means of support for generations to come. What is most inspirational of all is that Margaret Rudkin was able to combine the roles of mother and businesswoman with such wonderful success.

Nancy Skarmeas is a book editor and mother of a newborn son, Gordon, who is keeping her and her husband quite busy at their home in New Hampshire. Her Greek and Irish ancestry has fostered a lifelong interest in research and history.

Treasures Beyond Measure

John C. Bonser

If we could reach up in the sky
And gather all the stars that lie
Like diamonds on a moon-lit floor,
Our mother's deeds would sparkle more!

If we could race through outer space
To find that "ivory-palace place,"
Our journey would be futile miles;
For heaven's near in Mother's smiles.

If oyster beds in oceans deep
Gave up the precious pearls they keep;
If earth's high hills revealed the ore
Gold miners have not found before,
Those pearls below, that gold above,
Would pale beside our mother's love!

Our Home

Kay Hoffman

Our home was one of simple style
  With a dear and cozy look;
It had the warmth of Mother's love
  In every little nook.

Lace doilies and lace tablecloth
  Crocheted by Mother's hand
Were placed with loving care upon
  Each table and each stand.

But more than things our eyes could see
  Within that home held dear
Was comfort that it brought to us
  To have our mother near.

When heartaches came and teardrops fell,
  We knew we could endure;
For Mother held us up in prayer,
  Her faith was strong and sure.

Though years have passed, I often go
  Back through kind mem'ry's door
To visit that old home again;
  And Mother's there once more.

Mama's Room

Carol Bessent Hayman

Mama's room was always the big front bedroom just to the left as you entered the two-story frame house with its sprawling porches on three sides, upstairs and down. Somehow we always gravitated there, and it became more living room to us than the parlor across the hall or the dining room with its wrought-iron day bed behind the parlor.

Each morning, Mama fluffed her big feather bed—the focal point of the room—into a cloudy mass and topped it with two snowy white feather pillows. Mama was very particular about her bed. You did not sit or loll about on it; and it was a treat of treats to get to sleep in this confection, which always felt just as good as it looked.

An assortment of furniture clustered around the bed, but I remember best Mama's dresser, which held her comb, brush, and mirror and an array of perfume and cologne bottles. If Mama had a weakness, it was for smelling good. "English Lavender" and "Evening in Paris" were her favorites, and each Christmas and birthday saw her stock replenished.

Several rocking chairs waited nearby, one of which we referred to as "Mama's chair"; and when the day's work ended and she could rest, we always knew we could find her here. It was here that I came with my confidences and my problems, and it was here that I brought my little joys and sorrows; for nothing seemed complete until it had been shared with Mama. She always listened as if each word I said had importance, and her opinion was always wise and full of love for me.

Mother

D. A. Hoover

Mem'ries bring me cradle days
Up from childhood's falt'ring ways—

How she kissed my tears away,
Nursed my bruises gained at play.

Nighttime silence chill and damp,
With her little bedside lamp,

Like an angel to my room,
She brought comfort in the gloom.

Prayed for me at start of day,
Watched me, thoughtless, grow away;

Sadness came to etch her face
When I left the old homeplace.

Now her principles and creeds
Follow me in all my deeds.

If some mark I make in life
Rises from our constant strife

And makes some noble effort grow,
Mother's hand has made it so.

IN THE MORNING
Boris Mihajlovic Kustodiev, 1878-1927
Russian State Museum, St. Petersburg, Russia
Superstock

Country
CHRONICLE
—Lansing Christman—

REMEMBER MOTHER

May is a lovely time of year to honor mothers. Mother birds flutter from limb to limb, bringing food to their young and whistling their soothing lullabies. The meadows and woodlands have softly put on their green, and the tilled fields mellow in the spring sunshine.

Perhaps the sweetest gifts of May are the beauty and perfume of the springtime flowers. As I stroll down one of my favorite paths, magnolias and honeysuckles fill the air with their sweet fragrance. I delight in the lilacs washed in purple and white and pink along the dooryard hedges, and the blooms of the peach and apple orchards paint the hills in glorious pastels.

Flowers are a beautiful way to celebrate mothers—one of God's greatest gifts! Mothers add so much love and care to life and home. They give their encouragement and guidance, their compassion and love. Because they offer such precious gifts, mothers should be honored with equally special gifts from nature; and a corsage of spring blooms is a perfect expression of love.

As each new May offers its abundant flowers to mothers both old and new, I urge everyone to take a moment to remember Mother. Such memories are truly precious. We cling to these remembrances of Mother just as when we were tiny toddlers years ago we held to her apron strings.

The author of two published books, Lansing Christman has been contributing to Ideals *for over twenty years. Mr. Christman has also been published in several American, foreign, and braille anthologies. He lives in rural South Carolina.*

Where Mother Was Born

Harriet Feltham

Deep in the country
    'Neath God's changing sky,
Where nature runs rampant
    And brilliant birds fly,

There nestles a cottage
    All weathered and worn,
That dear, little cottage
    Where Mother was born.

There hollyhocks grew
    Round the high picket fence
And old berry bushes
    Are matted and dense.

A big rambling rose
    Climbs over the door,
And I dream it's the same
    As it was years before

When we youngsters would play
    'Neath the shade of the trees
And wander through wildflowers
    Up to our knees.

And time cannot dim
    Those memories of yore;
They'll seem just the same
    As they were years before.

With picnics and baseball
    Under the trees,
No dreams are as cherished
    And loved more than these.

And they'll grow with the years
    And seem oh so fair,
Enhanced by the thought
    That my mother lived there.

WILDFLOWER COTTAGE
Eaton, New Hampshire
Dick Dietrich Photography

My Mother's Hands

Reginald Holmes

My mother's hands are clever hands
That cook and sew and clean;
And yet they never seem to tire
Of everyday routine.

She goes about her work with pride;
   And though her day is long,
She always keeps her heart in tune
   And lifts her voice in song.

My mother's hands are helping hands
   To those who are in need.
She always thinks of other folks
   And strives by words and deed

To lift the fallen, cheer the faint,
   And give them hope anew;
To show them that beneath each cloud,
   There lies a patch of blue.

My mother's hands are wrinkled now;
   But in each deep-etched line,
I read the history of her life
   And clasp those hands in mine.

To My First Love, My Mother

Christina G. Rossetti

Sonnets are full of love, and this my tome
    Has many sonnets: so here now shall be
    One sonnet more, a love sonnet, from me
To her whose heart is my heart's quiet home,
    To my first Love, my mother, on whose knee
I learnt love-lore that is not troublesome;
    Whose service is my special dignity,
And she my lodestar while I go and come.
And so because you love me, and because
    I love you, Mother, I have woven a wreath
      Of rhymes wherewith to crown your
        honored name:
      In you not fourscore years can dim the flame
Of love, whose blessed glow transcends the laws
    Of time and change and mortal life and death.

Mother

Ruth H. Underhill

You'd always find her busy
As she'd flit from room to room,
And hardly can I picture her
Without a mop or broom!

She kept the floors so shiny;
You could almost see your face.
And each and every trinket
Was dusted in its place.

Though constantly kept toiling
By the work of each new day,
She still had time to read to us
When we'd rest from our play.

She still had time to tuck us in
And hear our childish prayer;
The golden memories of Mother
Still hover everywhere!

Mending

Rebecca M. Brown

She always mended broken things:
Bud vases, dolls, and sparrow's wings.
I wonder, does she now bend down
To mend a cherub's broken crown?

She showed me loveliness each day:
The sparkling frost, the buds of May.
Does she now show sweet paradise
To newborn angels' wandering eyes?

If there's a rent in sky's deep blue,
A child of heav'n might just slip through.
Does she take needle, thread of gold
And sew it fast with a nice, neat fold?

Oh, I know she couldn't idle be
And even in heav'n's immensity
Is serving still, in her soul's rebirth,
The Master she so loved on earth.

ANNA'S HUMMINGBIRD. California. Superstock.

Window Air Show

Louise Pugh Corder

On both sides of the window screen,
Small, special beauties can be seen—
At the feeder, hummingbirds awhirl;
Inside with Grandma, a baby girl

BROAD-TAILED HUMMINGBIRD (MALE). Colorado. Superstock.

Enchanted by rotating wings
On the flashing, feathered, jeweled things.
Swift, tiny birds whir down and up,
Sipping from each flowerlike cup,

Helicopting unaware
Of the captivating child this fair.
No dazzling hummingbirds can glow
Like the big blue eyes that watch them so!

I Remember Grandma

Marlene M. Moore

I remember Grandma: the sweet smells of her kitchen, her coal-burning furnace, the walnut tree in her front yard, her weary climb up the stairs when the day was done. She was a heavy woman often clad in a cotton dress and starched apron, cottony brown nylons, and black lace-up shoes, her silver hair in a modest bun at the nape of her neck, encased with a hairnet. At night, those silver strands hung to her waist in a braid.

My brother and sister, Ron and Charla, and I remember well the hours Grandma spent in the kitchen baking pies, bread, and cookies to share with her neighbors or sell to the bakeries in town.

Today, Grandma's cupboard would be considered an antique, with its pull-out metal leaf, flour bin on the side, and storage space on both top and bottom for spices, dishes, and silverware. But to us three youngsters, it was a magical place where Grandma played in white stuff and made wonderful things to eat. Our favorite was her sugar cookies—a treat made especially for us.

Grandma lived in the country on a small farm. Her house sat on a hill, surrounded by pastureland where she raised a cow and a few chickens. Brilliant red poppies were planted on one side of the house, not far from the kitchen window.

A little distance behind the house stood a long low shed that housed the livestock. The shed leaned slightly, its timbers blackened from years of weather. Its tin roof rustled when the wind blew, echoing ominous sounds on cold winter nights and sparking my avid imagination.

While visiting Grandma's farm, we children faced the often daunting task of helping with the chores. The cow had to be brought from the pasture and milked, and the eggs had to be gathered.

Grandma milked Bossie while Ron and Charla and I went to gather the eggs. This was difficult since the rooster would often chase us, but the three of us braved his fury together, knowing that Grandma's cookies would be our reward.

When Grandma was done milking Bossie, it was our job to operate the separator, separating the cream from the milk. Switching turns without getting a hard wallop from the crank was no small feat, but we endured it for Grandma's cookies.

When the chores were done, Grandma was ready to bake. She'd reach high in the cupboard and bring down a large, glass tumbler, the only one big enough to cut our cookies. Slowly, with hands swollen and painful from arthritis, Grandma worked her miracle.

She mixed the ingredients in a large crock. Not by measurements, but by a pinch of this, a handful of that, and a little of this for taste. Grandma sprinkled flour on the metal leaf and skillfully rolled the dough out to the right thickness. She used the special tumbler to push gently through the pillowy dough and cut perfectly round shapes. Only eight cookies would fit on a baking sheet; they were so big. When Grandma placed the treats in the oven, it was time for us to get ready.

At just the right moment we would clamor around the oak table in the dining room with freshly washed hands, climb up onto the spindle-backed chairs, and wait patiently for our cookies. Moments later Grandma would announce their readiness with, "Now be careful, these are hot." A dish towel was put in place and the baking sheet carefully laid on it. Our mouths watered in anticipation.

Grandma served cookies to each of us and headed back to the kitchen to keep a watchful eye on the next batch. We would gobble down our first cookie and be well into the second by the time the next batch came. Three was our limit with both Grandma and our tummies, but the growing mound of steaming cookies gave assurance as to our treat for the next few days.

Yes, I remember Grandma.

She milked the cow, she beat her rugs on the clothesline, she plucked chickens for Sunday dinners, she babysat her grandchildren. And she made sugar cookies.

Springtime on the Farm

Velora Norwood Pease

The meadowlark is calling
    To his mate across the rye.
The west wind softly whispers
    As it passes slowly by
En route to greet the morning sun
    That mounts the eastern sky.

The dewdrops shine and sparkle
    On the fence and grass and trees.
The tulip nods and lifts its head
    To the caressing breeze
While all around I hear the humming
    Of the honeybees.

The apple orchard's laden
    With a wealth of perfume sweet.
A rabbit dashes past me
    On its timid, noiseless feet;
The bobolink is telling
    Of his nest among the wheat.

The lilac bushes with their weight
    Of purple clusters bend.
The lilies of the valley
    And the honeysuckle lend
Their beauty to the morning
    And their fragrance to the wind.

O springtime, lovely springtime!
    You do bring back memories
Of spring mornings long ago.
    Once again I feel the breeze
And smell the pungent odor
    Of the plum and apple trees.

SPRINGTIME ON THE FARM
East Corinth, Vermont
Dick Dietrich Photography

Spring
from Stillmeadow Sampler

Gladys Taber

The hyacinths I picked today smelled sweet and cool. But they looked so tropical, I could hardly believe it was a May morning in New England. The heavy spikes of purple and pink and ivory would fit some garden on a coral isle where there are no seasons at all, but it is forever summer. As I gathered just enough for a bouquet in the milk glass swan compote, I stopped to listen to the flickers down by the pond, and to watch a towhee in the feeder. The flickers have a dramatic call, "Wick, wick, wick," and the males always look as if they were dressed for a costume party in their grey, brown, white, and bright yellow with the scarlet crescent on the neck and black crescent on the breast. As they hammer away on tree trunks, they often brace themselves with their tails, and if they feel in the mood, they can hammer right through an eaves trough too.

The towhee is a shy bird, and calls for admiration when he comes so near the house. In his black and white and cinnamon-brown suit, he is handsome and I love to hear him saying, "Drink your teeeeee."

As I went back to the house, the sound of the lawn mower drowned out the rap-rap of the flickers. Somehow the first mowings are especially lovely, for the grass smells better than any perfume and the clippings fall green and thick behind the blades.

TRAVELER'S Diary

Laura K. Griffis

A GARDEN OF BAYOU BEND. Photograph courtesy of the Museum of Fine Arts, Houston, Texas. Rick Gardner, photographer.

THE BAYOU BEND COLLECTION AND GARDENS
Houston, Texas

A lacy, green canopy of leaves shields me from the Texas sun as I cross the footbridge leading to Bayou Bend Collection and Gardens. Through the weathered wooden planks, I catch a glimpse of the bayou below. The narrow stream of water winds through a lush carpet of ferns and ivy. At the end of the footbridge, tangled plants and vines give way to a neatly manicured courtyard. Resisting the temptation to scoop up a handful of pink azalea blossoms, I move through the garden toward the museum. To my surprise, I see an elegant house presiding over a rolling green lawn that does not look like a museum at all. I have come to Bayou Bend.

The lady of this charming house no longer lives here; but her vivacious spirit remains, as does her rare collection of American antiques. The daughter of a Texas governor, James Stephan Hogg, Miss Ima Hogg spent her life building one of America's most treasured collections of antiques. As a girl growing up in the governor's mansion, Miss Hogg developed an appreciation for tasteful surroundings and a knack for hosting guests. She dreamed of pursuing these interests into adulthood. The culmination of her efforts, Bayou Bend Mansion, was completed in 1920. During her lifetime, she opened the doors of her home to the public, inviting others to share her fondness for American works of art.

Entering through the Folk Art Porch, I feel like one of Miss Hogg's personal guests. A wooden statue of an Indian princess bids me welcome, her hand raised in a delicate gesture of greeting. I admire the rustic collection of folk artifacts, from the rooster-shaped weather vane to the carved American eagle with outstretched wings.

The next room I enter represents the Pilgrim era. In the middle of the room stands the "Great Chair" which was reserved for the head of the household or the guest of honor. Because few colonists could afford more than one chair, other members of the household sat on benches or stools.

Objects throughout the house reflect the early-American desire to imitate European aristocracy. For example, ornate wooden tea tables and delicate porcelain tea sets stand in the drawing room.

Moving into the front hallway, I catch a view of the mansion's front and back entrances. In the days before air-conditioning, these large doorways stood open to send a welcome, velvety breeze floating through the house. Visitors entering through the front doorway could see past the elegantly curved staircase to a beautiful, sparkling fountain in the backyard.

BAYOU BEND, SOUTH FACADE AND GARDENS (top, Rick Gardner, photographer) and QUEEN ANNE SITTING ROOM (bottom). Photographs courtesy of the Museum of Fine Arts, Houston, Texas.

Since its completion, an array of prominent people have visited Bayou Bend. Even after Miss Hogg's death in 1975, the house continued to serve as an elegant spot for entertaining. President George Bush once hosted a stately dinner here for foreign dignitaries. The antique dining room with its gilded wallpaper provided a luxurious backdrop for modern-day diplomacy.

While the dining room displays splendor and refinement, other rooms in the house have a more rustic flavor. A Quaker preacher named Edward Hicks painted the folk picture that hangs above the fireplace in a cozy upstairs bedroom. Miss Hogg chose it for her collection because she loved the subject matter: the peaceable kingdom from Isaiah 11.

Miss Hogg's eye for beauty did not stop within the house itself, a fact of which I'm reminded as I step outside into a spring garden bursting with pink, red, and salmon-colored azaleas. Winding my way through the wooded paths and flowering courtyards, I stumble upon the White Garden, a heavenly area blanketed with sugary white tulips and snowy azaleas.

Nearing the footbridge once again, I turn for a last look at Miss Hogg's idyllic homestead. Nestled next to the bayou, the house and gardens are an oasis of hospitality. The genteel lady who envisioned this museum had something unique in mind. Not only did she want to share her love for American art, she wanted to welcome each visitor as her personal guest. She succeeded in her task; leaving Bayou Bend, I feel as though I should send my hostess a thank-you note.

A native of Texas, Laura K. Griffis is finishing her senior year at Vanderbilt University while working as an Ideals editorial intern. Laura collects postcards from her travels to museums around the world as a part of her ongoing study of international cultures.

Cherry Trees

Stella Tremble

The trees are busy all year long
With leaves and fruit and flowers;
They entertain the birds and bees
Through fragrant, sunny hours.

Unselfish are they, pleased to give
For nests a hidden space,
In summertime beneath their arms
A cool and shady place.

They bow and visit with the winds,
Laugh softly with the breeze,
Then hold the sunlight as it shines
Upon the trembling leaves.

In spring, they throw a little shower
Of snowy blossoms white,
Caught by the tender grass below
Which holds them with delight.

CHERRY BLOSSOMS
Central Park, New York City
Kit Latham/FPG International

From My Garden Journal

by Deana Deck

PANSY

Early last fall, in a conversation with my best friend, Stephanie, I mentioned that I was preparing to set out my pansies. She commented that it didn't seem right to her to plant them in the fall, even though the garden centers were loaded with them. They were, she insisted, a spring flower and should remain so.

I understand her sentiments. Pansies are traditionally considered proof that spring has truly arrived. They are not only the first bedding plants I remember my mother setting out, they were the only flowers I remember her ever planting. Perhaps it was because the Army kept our family on the move too often to plant spring-flowering bulbs, so my mother faithfully celebrated the season by planting pansies in early spring. For most of my life, they were associated in my mind exclusively with that season. Then an interesting thing happened.

A few years back, I noticed that several nearby office parks had banks of colorful pansies blooming all winter. It was a cheerful sight in a climate where several gray weeks of forty-two degree temperatures and rain pretty much sum up winter. The following fall I decided to plant pansies in September. They bloomed beautifully until that week of frigid, real winter the Midsouth experiences in early January. At that point, they sort of shriveled up and disappeared. I was prepared to replant in the spring, but I never got the chance. While I was poking around the garden in mid-February, I noticed some fresh green growth and little stems with buds peeking out of the mulch. The pansies were waking. They bloomed nonstop until the middle of June when the southern sun finally got the best of them.

The real benefit, as I pointed out to Stephanie, is that the weather is so nice in September, and the soil so warm, that setting out bedding plants is truly a pleasure. Especially when compared to performing the same task in late February or early March with cold fingers, muddy boots, and bulky jackets reminding you that spring is still beyond the horizon. If your climate is snowbound several months of the year, you'll have to plant in late spring; but hopefully you can leave your bulky winter jacket inside.

Pansies are members in good standing of the *viola*, or violet family. In fact, all pansies are violas, although not all violas are pansies. Thanks to some adventurous horticulturists, pansies resulted from a crossbreeding between the wild, tri-color Johnny-jump-up (*Viola tri-color*), the perennial yellow-flowering *Viola lutea*, and a large, blue Dutch species, *Viola altaica*. Within a few years, breeders had developed a large, beauti-

PANSY

fully shaped flower with contrasting blotches on the petals—the familiar pansy "face." This first pansy was refined into the cultivar sold by garden centers everywhere: *Viola x wittrockiana*.

When pansies were introduced commercially in the mid-1800s, cottage gardeners were thrilled; yet the upper classes disdained the flowers as too gaudy. Nevertheless, by 1845 one magazine listed 354 named varieties of pansies.

Exceedingly popular with the Victorians, pansies declined in popularity during the era following the turn of the century; and by the end of World War II, few of the original cultivars remained. Pansies were available in only limited colors for several decades, but in recent years have made remarkable comeback, partly due to the more subtle colors being produced today.

Two specific developments have transformed the pansy garden. One was the introduction of the clear-faced, or nonblotched, varieties. These are known as Clear Crystal pansies and come in wonderful colors like pale sky blue, Swedish yellow, and soft sherbet-orange. The other development was a series in so-called "antique" colors, even though no ancient pansy ever sported these Monet-like blends of pastel pinks, ivories, yellows, and lavenders.

Another hybrid trait that has become quite popular is that of massive blooms. Known as Majestics, some of these flowers are three or more inches in diameter, many in rich, deep shades of blue, purple, and scarlet.

Although choosing from the variety of beautiful colors may be difficult, planting pansies is easy. They can be started indoors from seed if you live in a cold climate, or they can be planted directly into the garden in either very early spring or late summer. Where I live, we have so many cool-season weeds popping up in the garden that tiny pansy seedlings get lost in the shuffle. Since I have no space for starting them indoors, I just purchase bedding plants and set them out. Fall plants can be protected from winter's worst weather by a straw mulch or spun-polyester row covers.

Pansies are wonderfully trouble-free if your soil drains well. It's a good idea to condition the soil with some sand and compost along with a good all-purpose fertilizer if you have heavy clay in your area. Root rot brought about by standing in puddles will quickly put an end to your pansy bed.

Pansies are heavy feeders, so for maximum bloom, fertilize them every few weeks. Pluck the dead blossoms off the plants regularly to keep them blooming longer. When the weather gets hot around here, I usually just dig up the pansies and replace them with heat-tolerant annuals; but in climates with less torrid summers, they can be cut back once the flowers begin to fade, fed well, and left to rest until the weather turns cool again. They will immediately start putting out new shoots and buds, and you're all set for fall!

Here's an interesting tip: pansies are edible. The more fragrant the variety, the more tasty. They are useful as edible garnishes for salads, cakes, gelatin desserts, and cookies—in their natural state or crystallized. They are spectacular on wedding or birthday cakes; and when frozen within ice cubes, they can make ordinary summer lemonade truly special. Just be sure no dangerous chemicals were used in your soil or on your plants.

While pansies may continue to be a happy-faced harbinger of spring in your region, they have become a welcome delight in my Tennessee garden throughout fall, winter, and spring. I think of them as harbingers of happiness in my life. Now if I could just convince Stephanie!

Deana Deck lives in Nashville, Tennessee, where her popular garden column is a regular feature in The Tennessean.

Spring Bouquet

Kay Hoffman

The spring bouquet I'm sending you
Is not of flowers bright,
But of wishes that will linger
When blooms have taken flight.

I wish for you the bloom of health
To last your whole life through,
A work that is fulfilling,
And friendship warm and true.

I wish for you a prayer time
To keep your heart aware
Of the beauty of God's blessings
That fill the springtime air.

Unlike a May Day basket bright
I'd hang upon your door,
My spring bouquet of wishes
Will bloom forevermore.

VIOLAS, AZALEAS, CLEMATIS, AND NASTURTIUMS
Missouri Botanical Garden
St. Louis, Missouri
R. Todd Davis Photography

Readers' Forum

Meet Our Ideals Readers and Their Families

ATTENTION *IDEALS* READERS: The *Ideals* editors are looking for Favorite Mother's Day Memories for the magazine. Please send a typed description of your favorite memory to: Favorite Memories, c/o Editorial Department, Ideals Publications Inc., P.O. Box 305300, Nashville, Tennessee 37230.

Dear Reader,

I have some exciting news. Beginning with *Friendship Ideals* (published in August 1996), you will notice that your copy of *Ideals* is thicker. That's because we will be adding an additional eight pages to every issue so that we can bring you even more of the poems, photography, and inspiration of *Ideals*.

Specific plans for these additional pages call for each issue to feature two pages of a breathtaking scenic photograph from one of our country's magnificent spots; an inspiring feature entitled "My Favorite Memory," reminiscences of holidays and family life; "Devotions from the Heart," a special seasonal reflection on a Bible verse and its significance to everyday life; and "Our Heritage," a time-honored poem, speech, or story that reminds us of what it means to be an American. These additional features are only a part of our ongoing efforts to provide you with even more reasons to treasure *Ideals*.

And beginning in *1997*, *Ideals* will reach your mailbox approximately every other month as we begin publishing on a schedule of six issues per year: EASTER, MOTHER'S DAY, COUNTRY, FRIENDSHIP, THANKSGIVING, and CHRISTMAS. These thicker issues, filled with the same editorial excellence that you've come to expect from us, will still not contain any advertising.

I look forward to the opportunity of bringing you this larger and expanded magazine with the same publishing quality and reading pleasure our readers have enjoyed for more than fifty years. Thank you for your continued support.

Sincerely,

Patricia A. Pingry

Patricia A. Pingry
Publisher

ANN BUDD of Westland, Michigan, sent us this snapshot of her two great-granddaughters enjoying one another's company and the beautiful spring weather. Eighteen-month-old Addison and seven-month-old Olivia are the daughters of Melanie and Brian Parker. The Parkers live in nearby Dearborn, Michigan, so lucky Great-Grandma gets to visit with Addison and Olivia at least once a week. She is proud to say they are the light of her life!

MARY M. AUTHIER of Dearborn Heights, Michigan, praises the talent and beauty of her mother, Madeleine C. Authier. Madeleine, who celebrated her ninety-sixth birthday this spring, is pictured above with four of her thirteen great-grandchildren: Calvin Fadool of Boston, Massachusetts; and Andrea Montello, Christopher Lefaide, and Jeffrey Lefaide, all of Windsor, Ontario. As Mary and her two sisters were growing up, Madeleine, a gifted poet herself, loved to share the poetry of *Ideals* with them. She still loves to read from the magazine and has given all her children and grandchildren gift subscriptions of their own!

THANK YOU Mary M. Authier and Ann Budd for sharing with *Ideals*. We hope to hear from other readers who would like to share photos and stories with the *Ideals* family. Please include a self-addressed, stamped envelope if you would like the photos returned. Keep your original photographs for safekeeping and send duplicate photos along with your name, address, and telephone number to:

READERS' FORUM
IDEALS PUBLICATIONS INC.
P.O. BOX 305300
NASHVILLE, TENNESSEE 37230

ideals

Publisher, Patricia A. Pingry
Editor, Lisa C. Ragan
Copy Editor, Michelle Prater Burke
Electronic Prepress Manager, Amilyn K. Lanning
Editorial Intern, Laura K. Griffis
Contributing Editors, Lansing Christman, Deana Deck, Russ Flint, Pamela Kennedy, Patrick McRae, Mary Skarmeas, Nancy Skarmeas

ACKNOWLEDGMENTS

WHEN MOTHER MADE AN ANGEL CAKE from *THE PATH TO HOME* by Edgar A. Guest, copyright ©1919 by the Reilly & Lee Co. Used by permission of the author's estate. MAMA'S ROOM from *THESE LOVELY DAYS* by Carol Bessent Hayman, copyright ©1971 by Carol B. Hayman. Used by permission of the author. SPRING from *STILLMEADOW SAMPLER* by Gladys Taber, copyright ©1959 by Gladys Taber. Copyright renewed ©1987 by Constance Taber Colby. All rights reserved. Reprinted by permission of Brandt & Brandt Literary Agency, Inc. CHERRY TREES from *THORNS AND THISTLEDOWN* by Stella Craft Tremble, copyright ©1945 by Stella Tremble. Used by permission of the author's estate. Our sincere thanks to the following author whom we were unable to contact: Helen Welshimer for APRON STRINGS.

CELEBRATE AMERICA
AND RELIVE OUR GREAT HERITAGE
THROUGH THE PAGES OF IDEALS BOOKS

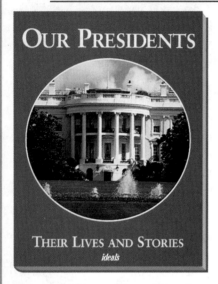

ORDER 3 COPIES OF THE SAME TITLE OR MIXED TITLES AND RECEIVE A FREE MYSTERY GIFT!

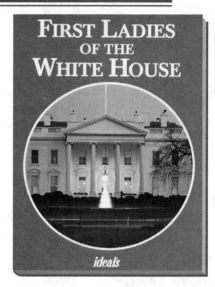

OUR PRESIDENTS—Biographies, photographs, and paintings of each of our 42 presidents. Eighty pages, laminated softcover, over 40 photographs. $7.95 (1127XA)

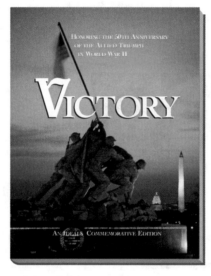

FIRST LADIES OF THE WHITE HOUSE Photographs, paintings, and biographies of each of our first ladies. Eighty pages, laminated softcover, over 40 photographs. $7.95 (40660A)

VICTORY—A tribute to the men and women who fought and died in World War II. Over 100 sepia-toned photographs along with short, nostalgic text. Eighty pages, laminated hardcover. $9.95 (40687A)

THE STORY OF AMERICA—The events that made our country great as told through photographs, poems, and paintings. Eighty pages, laminated softcover, over 40 photographs. $7.95 (11059A)

IDEALS BOOKS MAKE GREAT GIFTS. JUST USE THE ATTACHED FORM TO ORDER, AND WE'LL DO THE REST.

HEAR AMERICA SINGING—Words and music to 20 patriotic songs to sing and play. Illustrated with thrilling photographs and paintings. Eighty pages, laminated softcover, over 40 photographs. $7.95 (11172A)

Order now using the attached form, or call toll-free 1-800-558-4343.
We're sorry, but we are unable to ship orders outside the United States.